INVENTIONS AND DISCOVERY

# THE Z-BOYS
## AND SKATEBOARDING

BY JAMESON ANDERSON
ILLUSTRATED BY STEVE ERWIN

**Consultant:**
Michael Brooke, publisher
*Concrete Wave* magazine
Thornill, Ontario, Canada

Capstone
*press*

Mankato, Minnesota

Graphic Library is published by Capstone Press,
151 Good Counsel Drive, P.O. Box 669, Mankato, Minnesota 56002.
www.capstonepress.com

1 2 3 4 5 6 12 11 10 09 08 07

*Library of Congress Cataloging-in-Publication Data*
Anderson, Jameson.
  The Z-boys and skateboarding / by Jameson Anderson.
  p. cm.—(Graphic library. Inventions and discovery)
  Includes bibliographical references and index.
  ISBN-13: 978-1-4296-0150-4 (hardcover)
  ISBN-10: 1-4296-0150-7 (hardcover)
  1. Z-boys (Group) 2. Skateboarding—California. I. Title. II. Series.
GV859.8.A53 2008
796.22—dc22                                          2007004915

Summary: Describes the birth of the Z-boys skateboarding team and how they
    influenced modern skateboarding.

*Designer*
Jason Knudson

*Colorist*
Michael Kelleher

*Editors*
Donald Lemke & Mandy Robbins

# TABLE OF CONTENTS

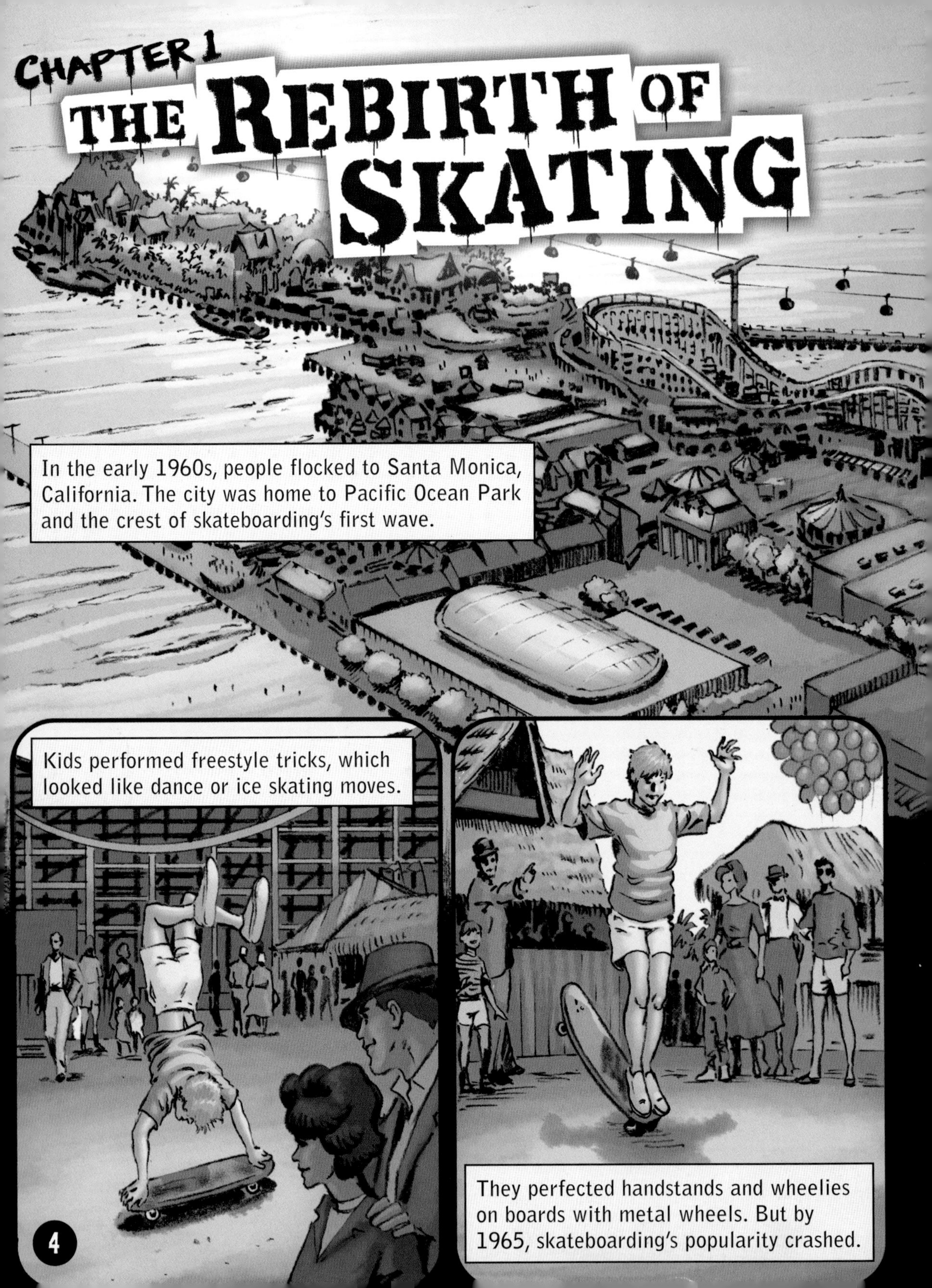

# CHAPTER 1

# THE REBIRTH OF SKATING

In the early 1960s, people flocked to Santa Monica, California. The city was home to Pacific Ocean Park and the crest of skateboarding's first wave.

Kids performed freestyle tricks, which looked like dance or ice skating moves.

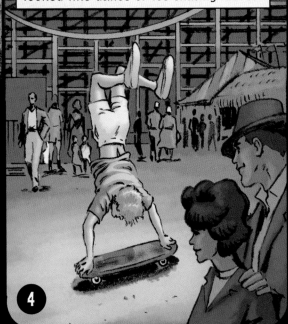

They perfected handstands and wheelies on boards with metal wheels. But by 1965, skateboarding's popularity crashed.

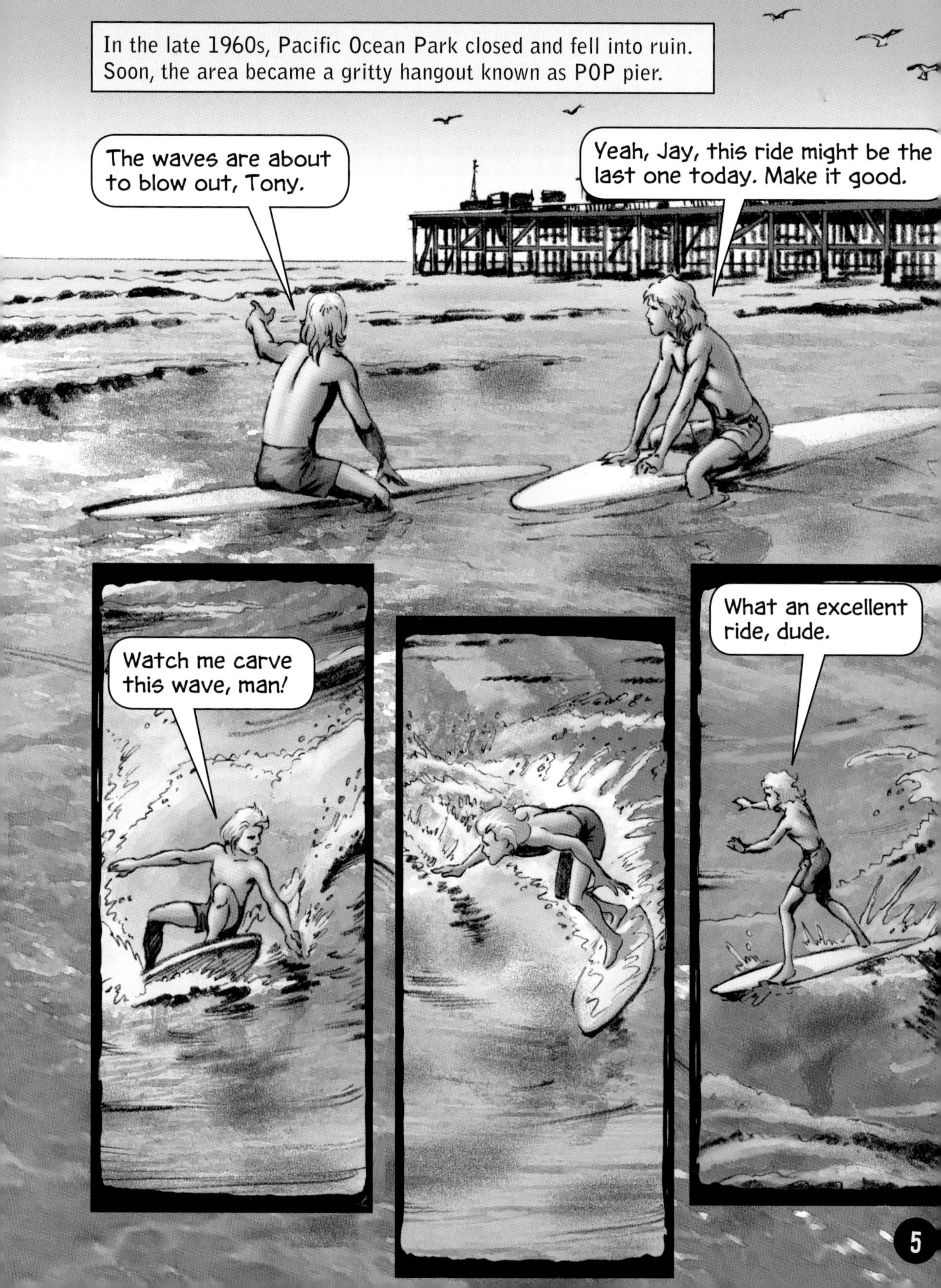
In the late 1960s, Pacific Ocean Park closed and fell into ruin. Soon, the area became a gritty hangout known as POP pier.
The waves are about to blow out, Tony.
Yeah, Jay, this ride might be the last one today. Make it good.
Watch me carve this wave, man!
What an excellent ride, dude.

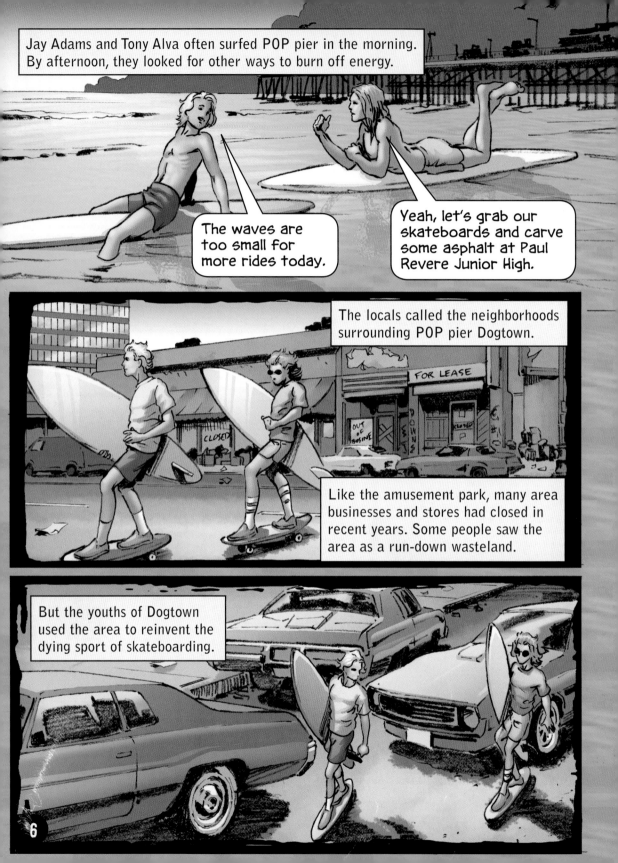

Jay Adams and Tony Alva often surfed POP pier in the morning. By afternoon, they looked for other ways to burn off energy.

The waves are too small for more rides today.

Yeah, let's grab our skateboards and carve some asphalt at Paul Revere Junior High.

The locals called the neighborhoods surrounding POP pier Dogtown.

Like the amusement park, many area businesses and stores had closed in recent years. Some people saw the area as a run-down wasteland.

But the youths of Dogtown used the area to reinvent the dying sport of skateboarding.

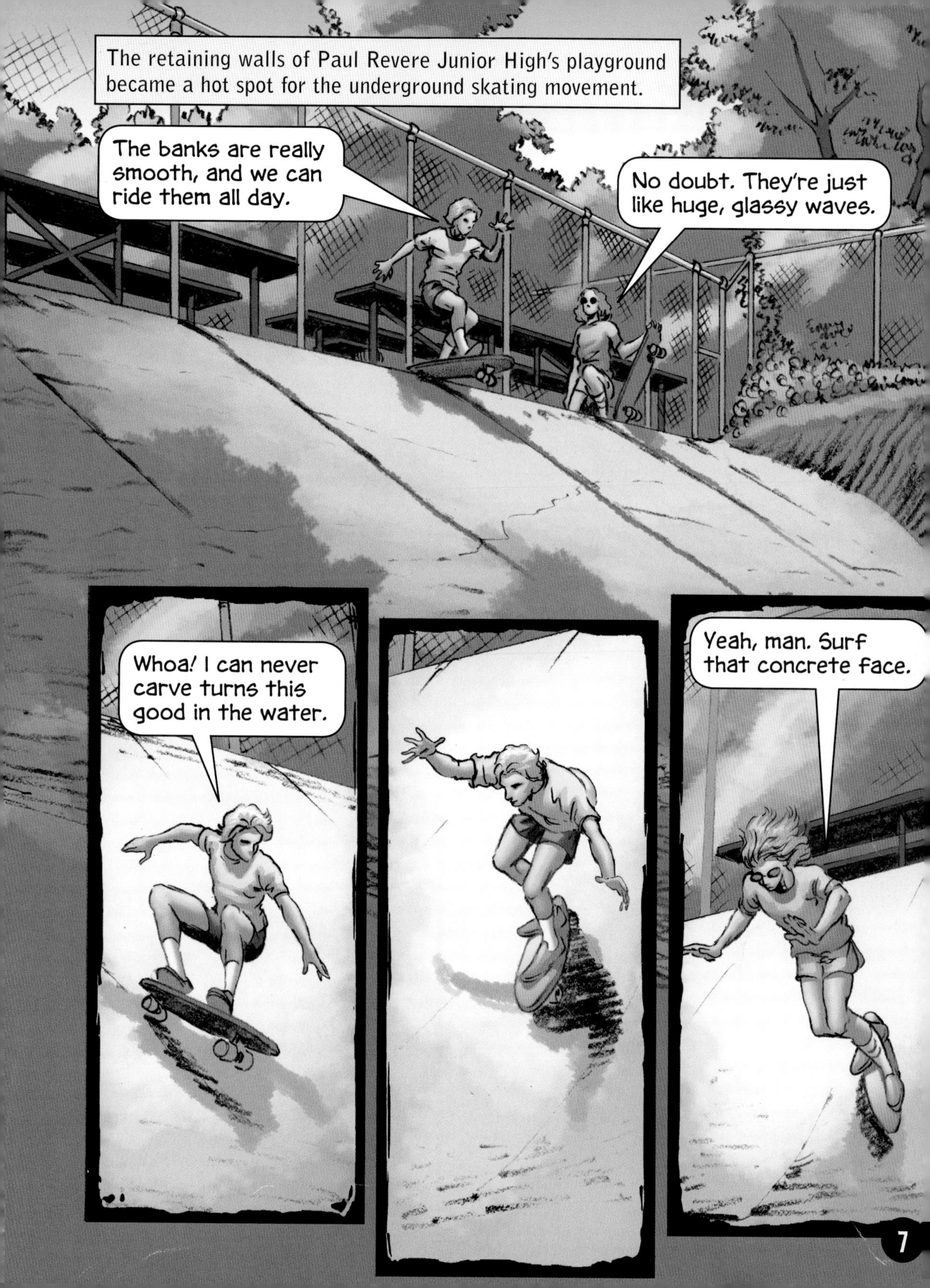
The retaining walls of Paul Revere Junior High's playground became a hot spot for the underground skating movement.
The banks are really smooth, and we can ride them all day.
No doubt. They're just like huge, glassy waves.
Whoa! I can never carve turns this good in the water.
Yeah, man. Surf that concrete face.

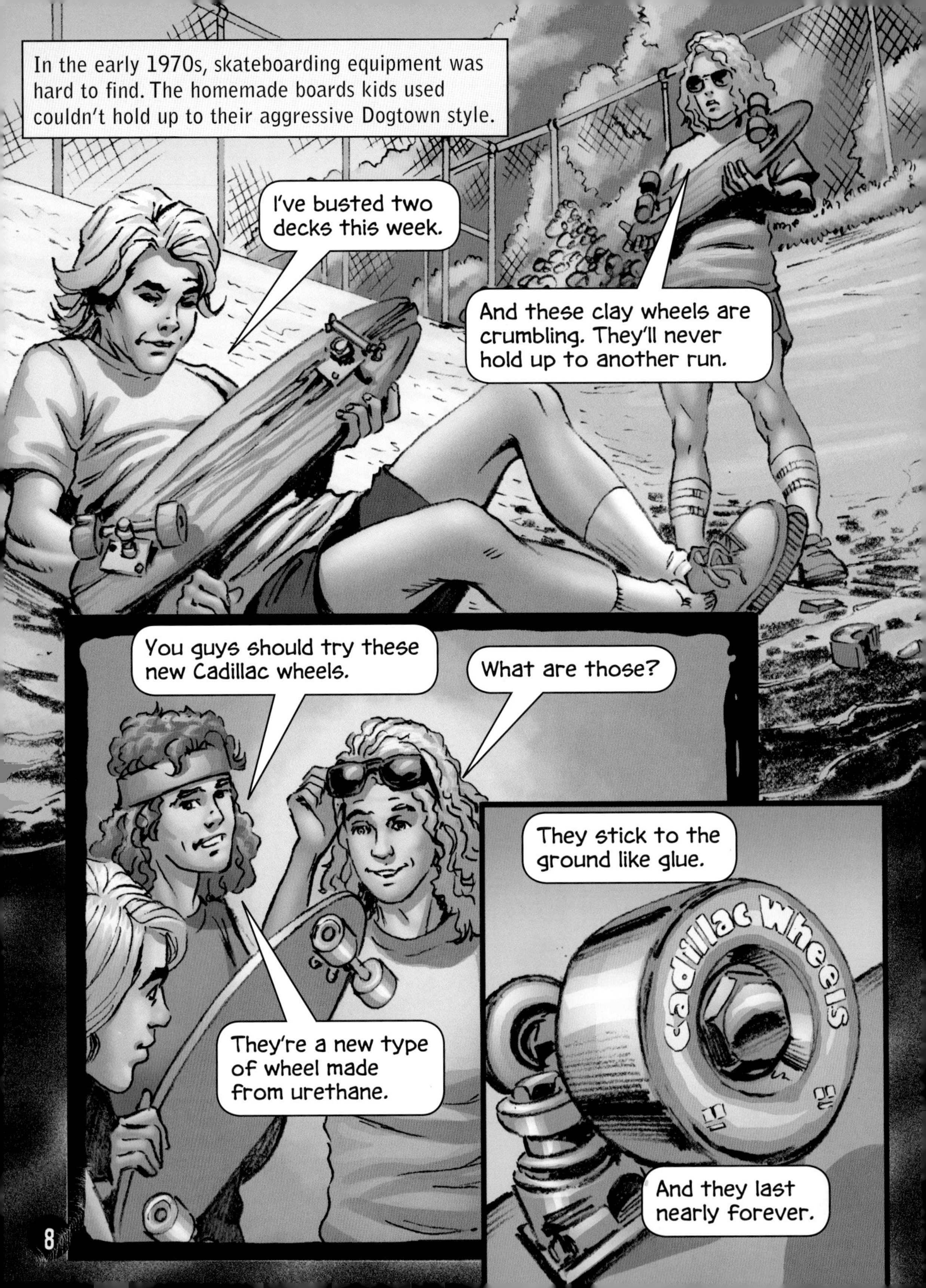
In the early 1970s, skateboarding equipment was hard to find. The homemade boards kids used couldn't hold up to their aggressive Dogtown style.
I've busted two decks this week.
And these clay wheels are crumbling. They'll never hold up to another run.
You guys should try these new Cadillac wheels.
What are those?
They're a new type of wheel made from urethane.
They stick to the ground like glue.
Cadillac Wheels
And they last nearly forever.

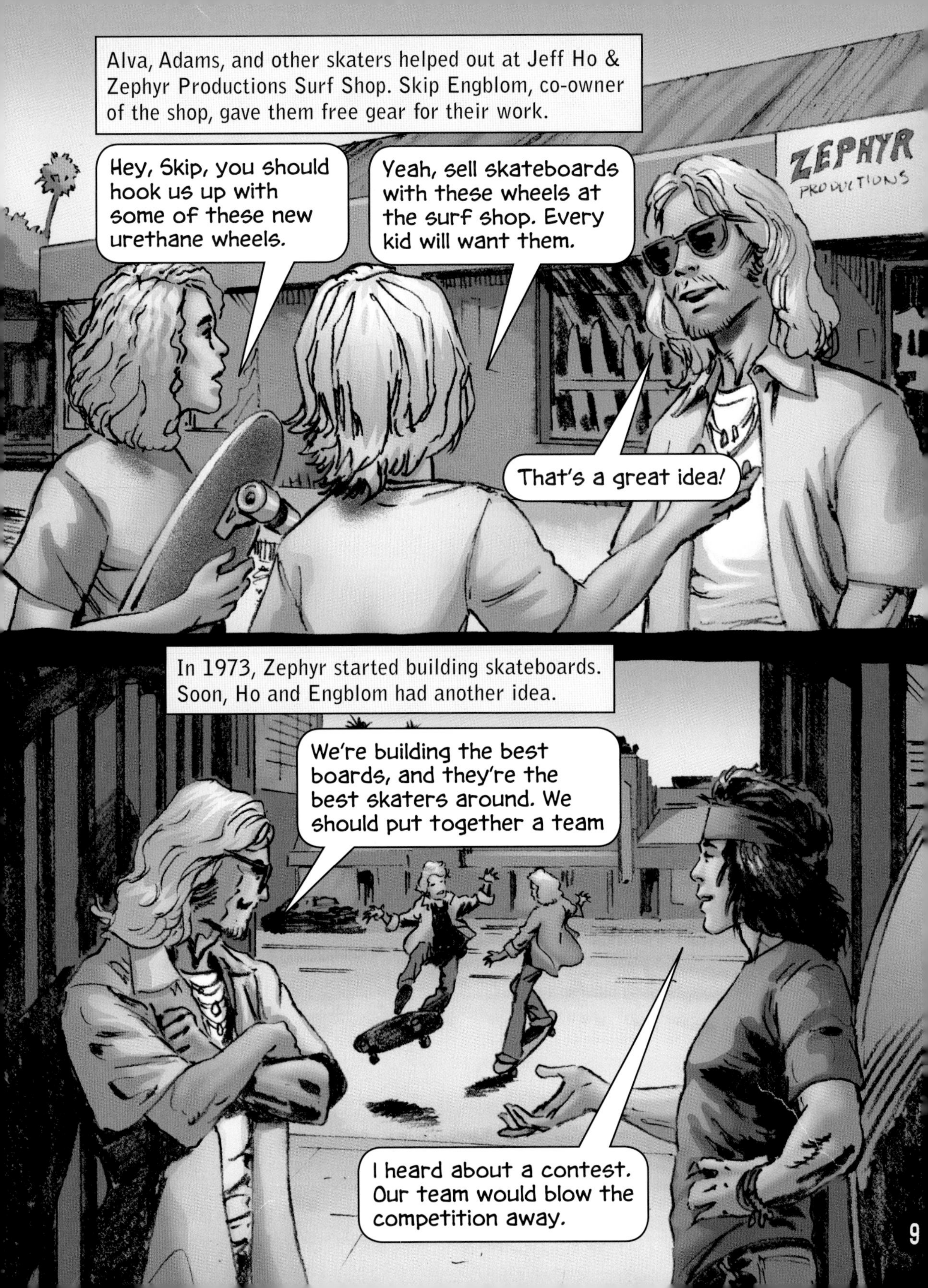
Alva, Adams, and other skaters helped out at Jeff Ho & Zephyr Productions Surf Shop. Skip Engblom, co-owner of the shop, gave them free gear for their work.
ZEPHYR PRODUCTIONS
Hey, Skip, you should hook us up with some of these new urethane wheels.
Yeah, sell skateboards with these wheels at the surf shop. Every kid will want them.
That's a great idea!
In 1973, Zephyr started building skateboards. Soon, Ho and Engblom had another idea.
We're building the best boards, and they're the best skaters around. We should put together a team
I heard about a contest. Our team would blow the competition away.

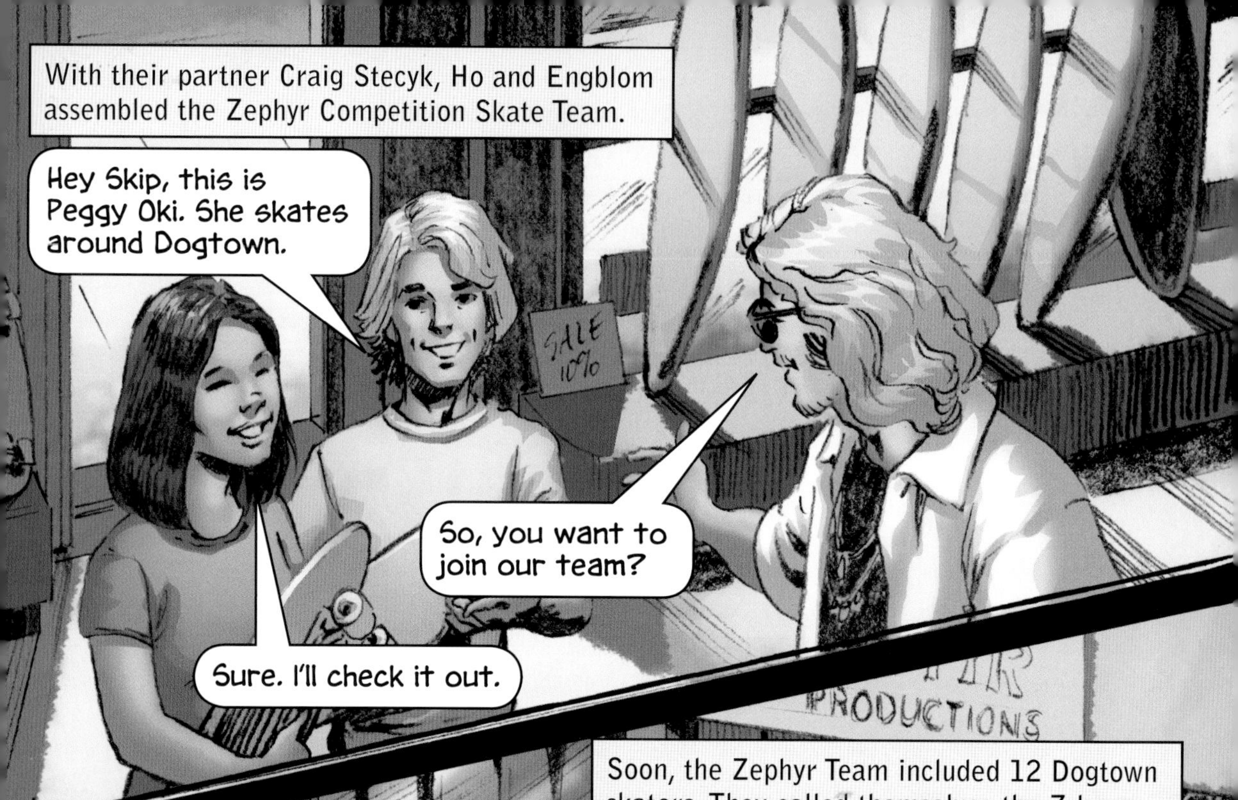
With their partner Craig Stecyk, Ho and Engblom assembled the Zephyr Competition Skate Team.
Hey Skip, this is Peggy Oki. She skates around Dogtown.
So, you want to join our team?
Sure. I'll check it out.
SALE 10%
PRODUCTIONS
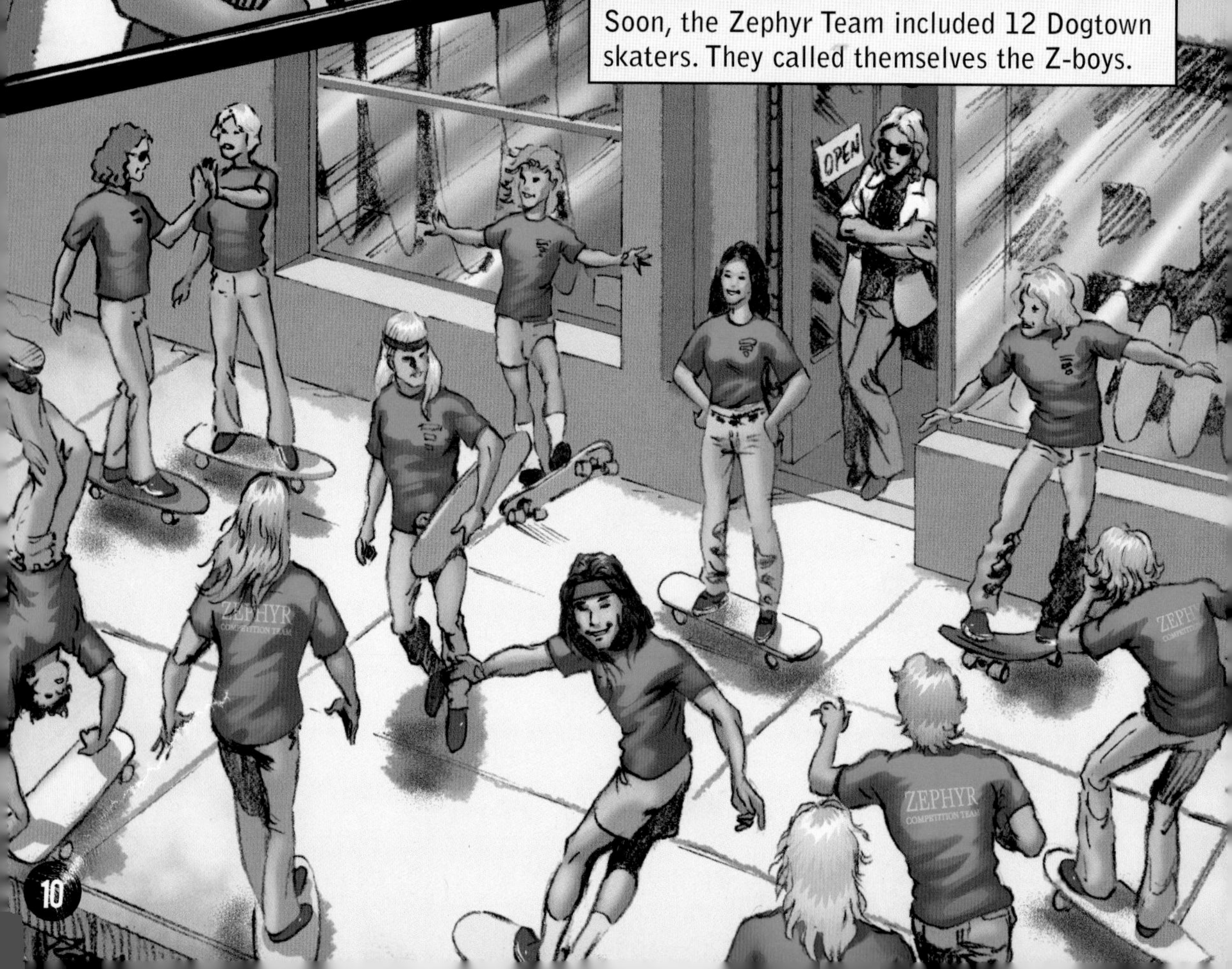
Soon, the Zephyr Team included 12 Dogtown skaters. They called themselves the Z-boys.
OPEN
ZEPHYR COMPETITION TEAM

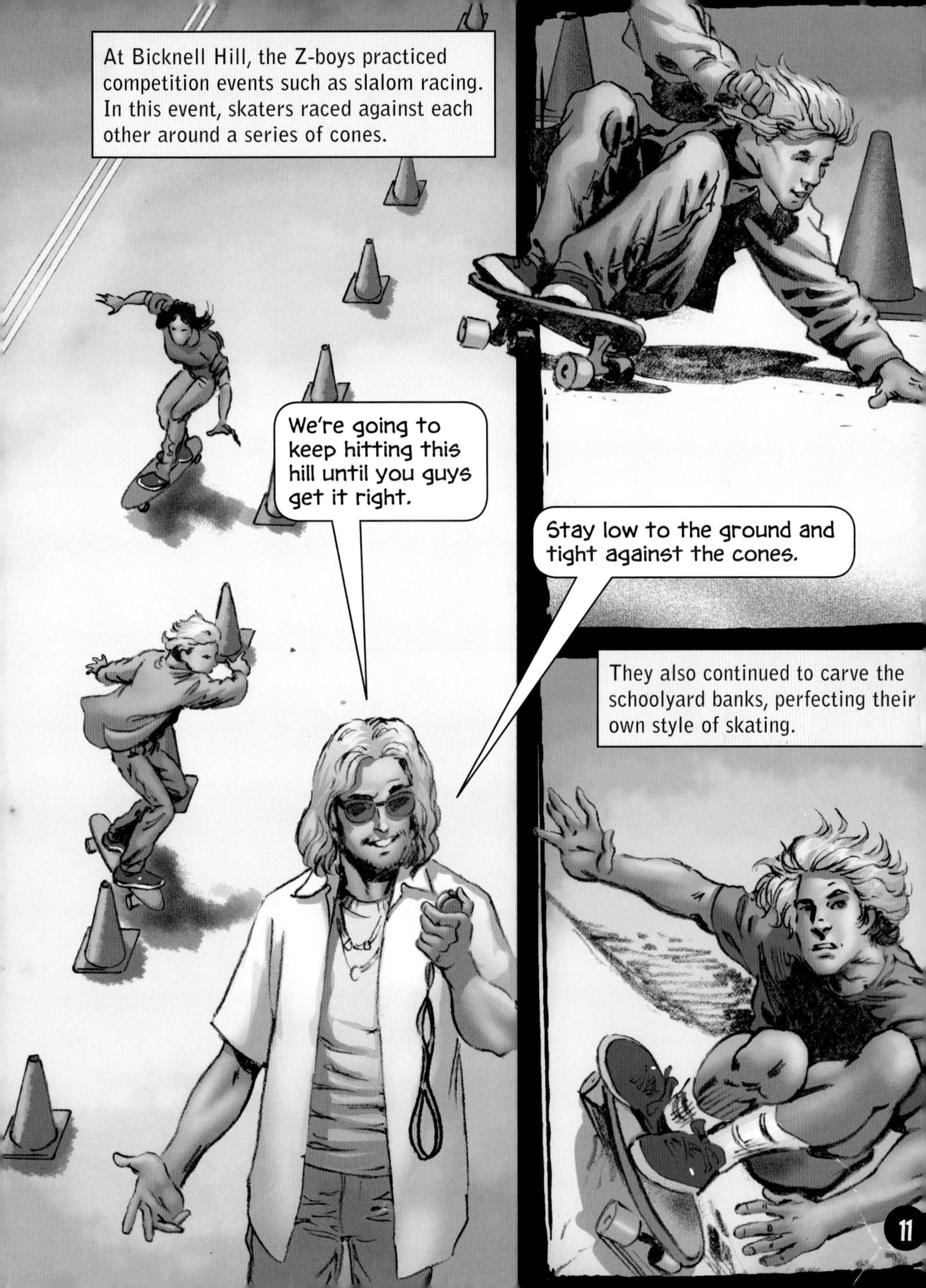
At Bicknell Hill, the Z-boys practiced competition events such as slalom racing. In this event, skaters raced against each other around a series of cones.
We're going to keep hitting this hill until you guys get it right.
Stay low to the ground and tight against the cones.
They also continued to carve the schoolyard banks, perfecting their own style of skating.

Chapter 2

# Competitions

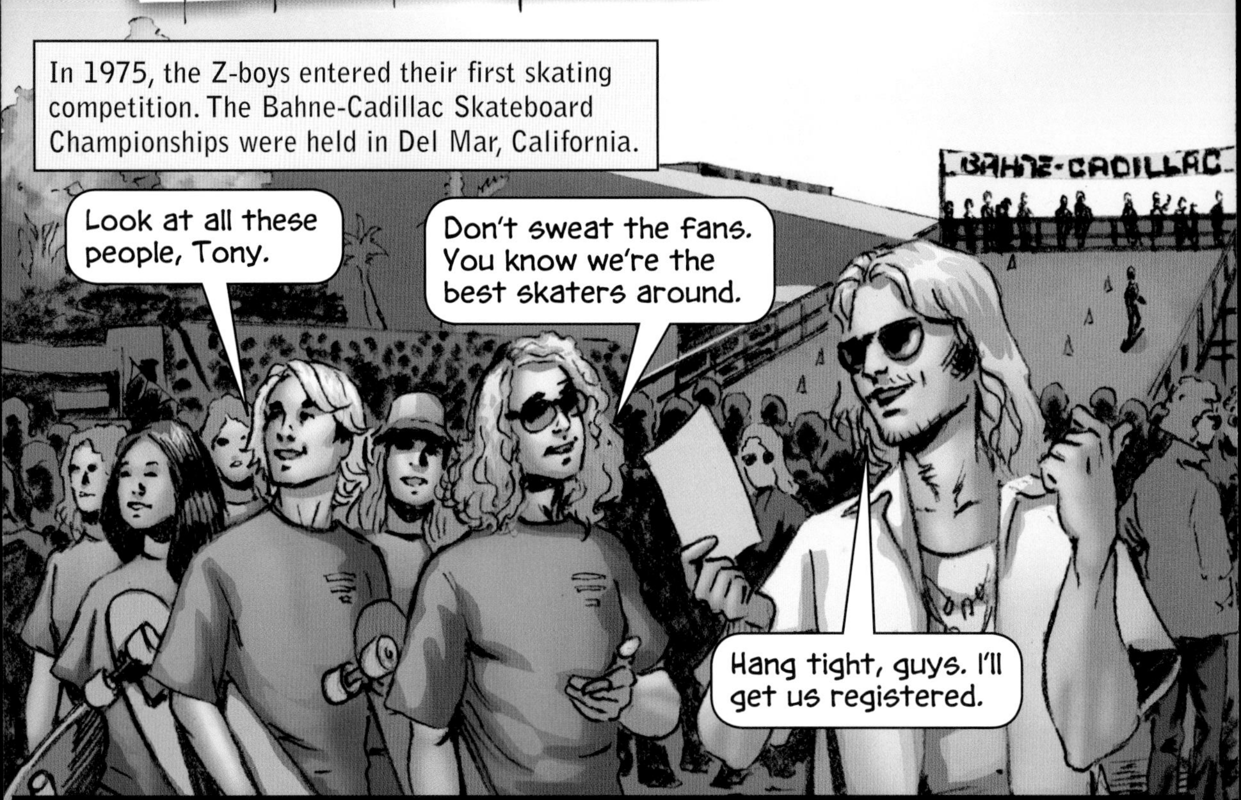
In 1975, the Z-boys entered their first skating competition. The Bahne-Cadillac Skateboard Championships were held in Del Mar, California.
BAHNE-CADILLAC
Look at all these people, Tony.
Don't sweat the fans. You know we're the best skaters around.
Hang tight, guys. I'll get us registered.

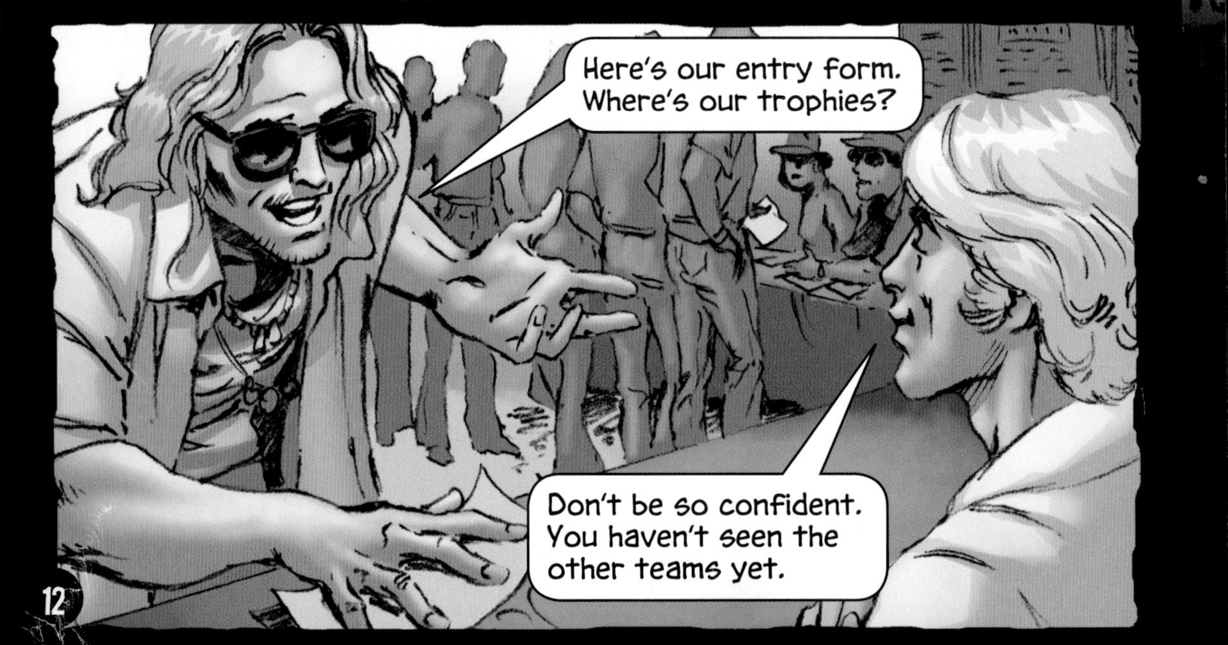
Here's our entry form. Where's our trophies?
Don't be so confident. You haven't seen the other teams yet.

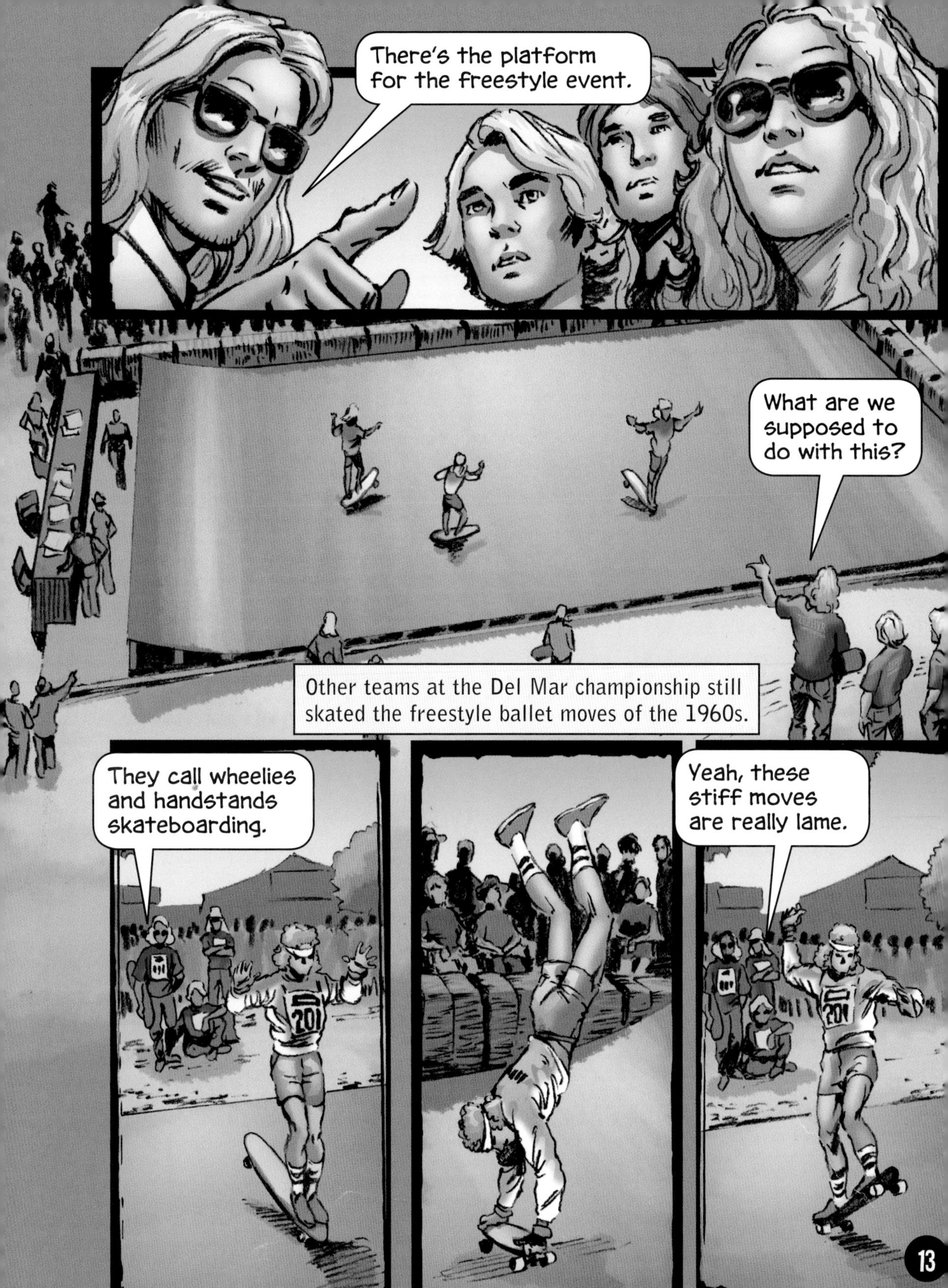
There's the platform for the freestyle event.
What are we supposed to do with this?
Other teams at the Del Mar championship still skated the freestyle ballet moves of the 1960s.
They call wheelies and handstands skateboarding.
Yeah, these stiff moves are really lame.
201
201

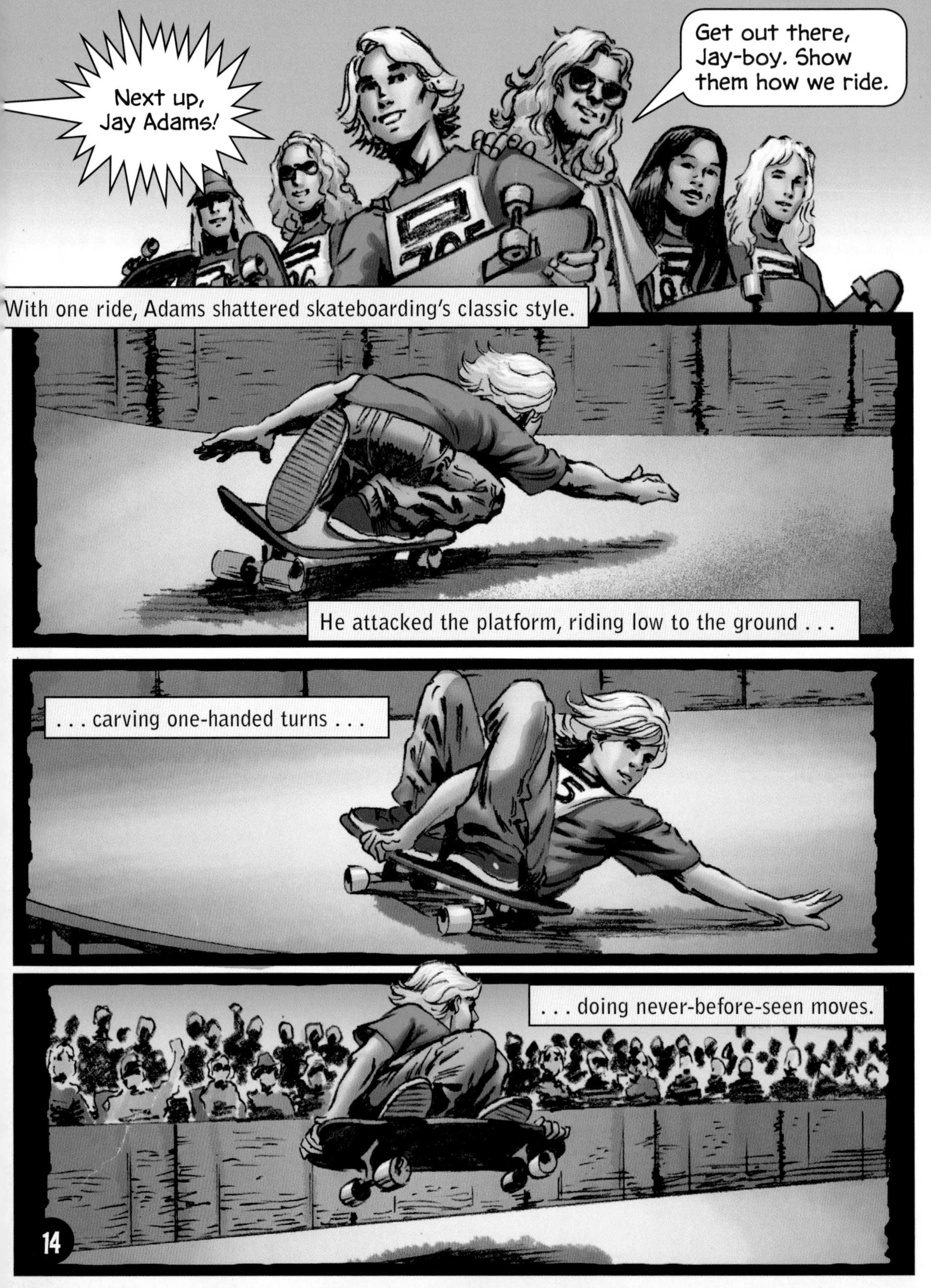
Next up, Jay Adams!
Get out there, Jay-boy. Show them how we ride.
With one ride, Adams shattered skateboarding's classic style.
He attacked the platform, riding low to the ground . . .
. . . carving one-handed turns . . .
. . . doing never-before-seen moves.

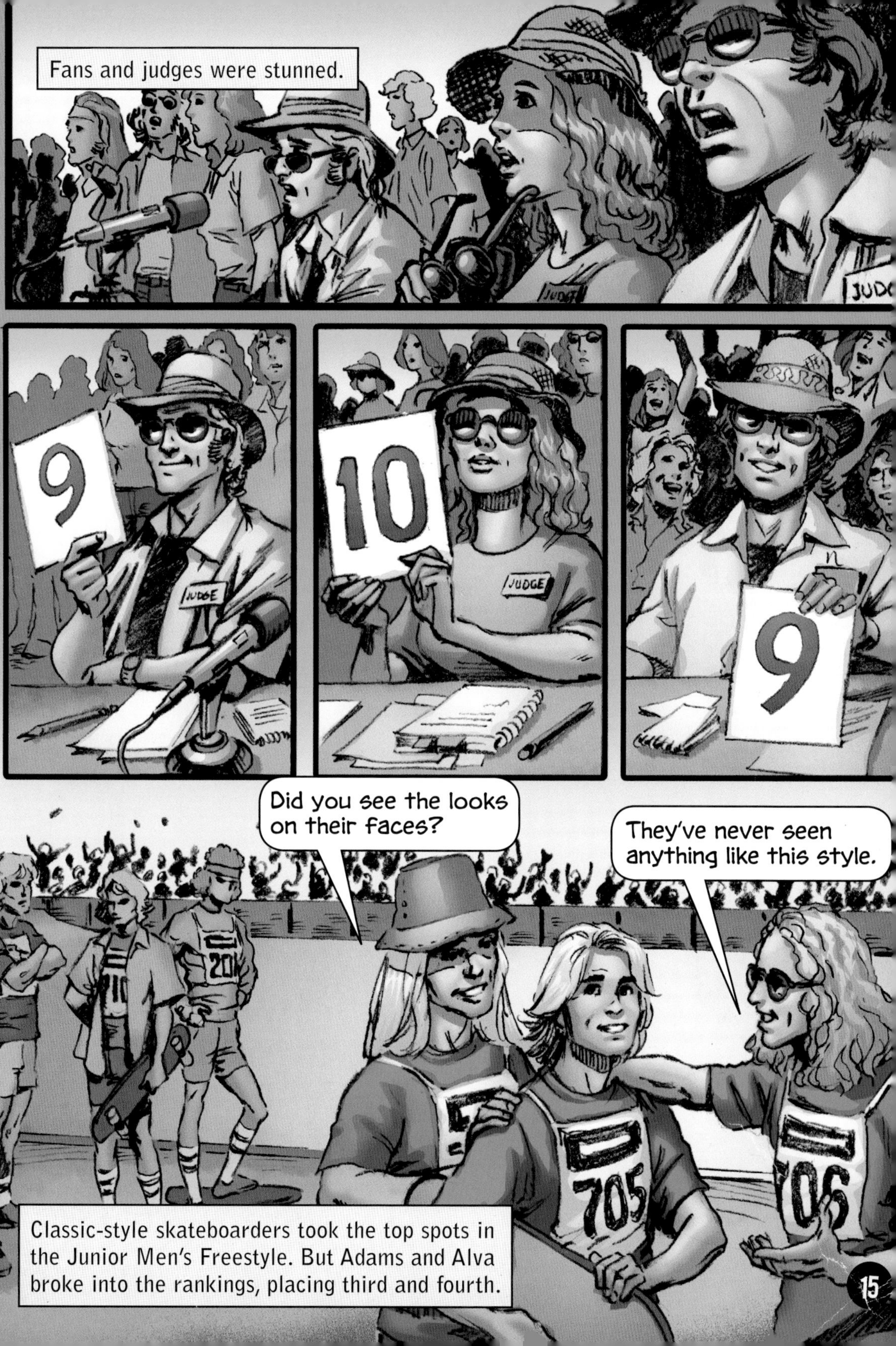
Fans and judges were stunned.
JUDGE
9
JUDGE
10
JUDGE
9
Did you see the looks on their faces?
They've never seen anything like this style.
705
Classic-style skateboarders took the top spots in the Junior Men's Freestyle. But Adams and Alva broke into the rankings, placing third and fourth.

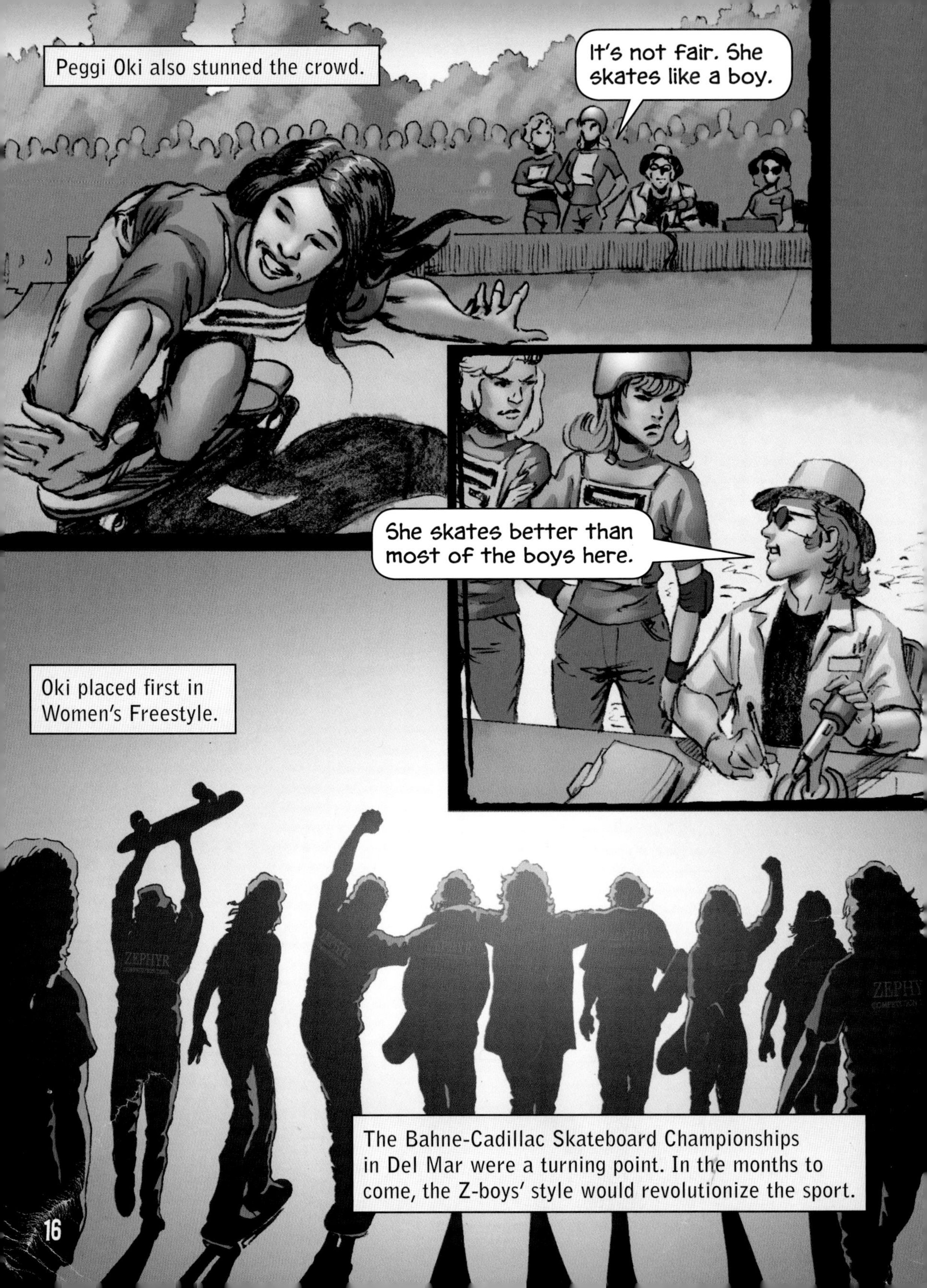
Peggi Oki also stunned the crowd.
It's not fair. She skates like a boy.
She skates better than most of the boys here.
Oki placed first in Women's Freestyle.
The Bahne-Cadillac Skateboard Championships in Del Mar were a turning point. In the months to come, the Z-boys' style would revolutionize the sport.

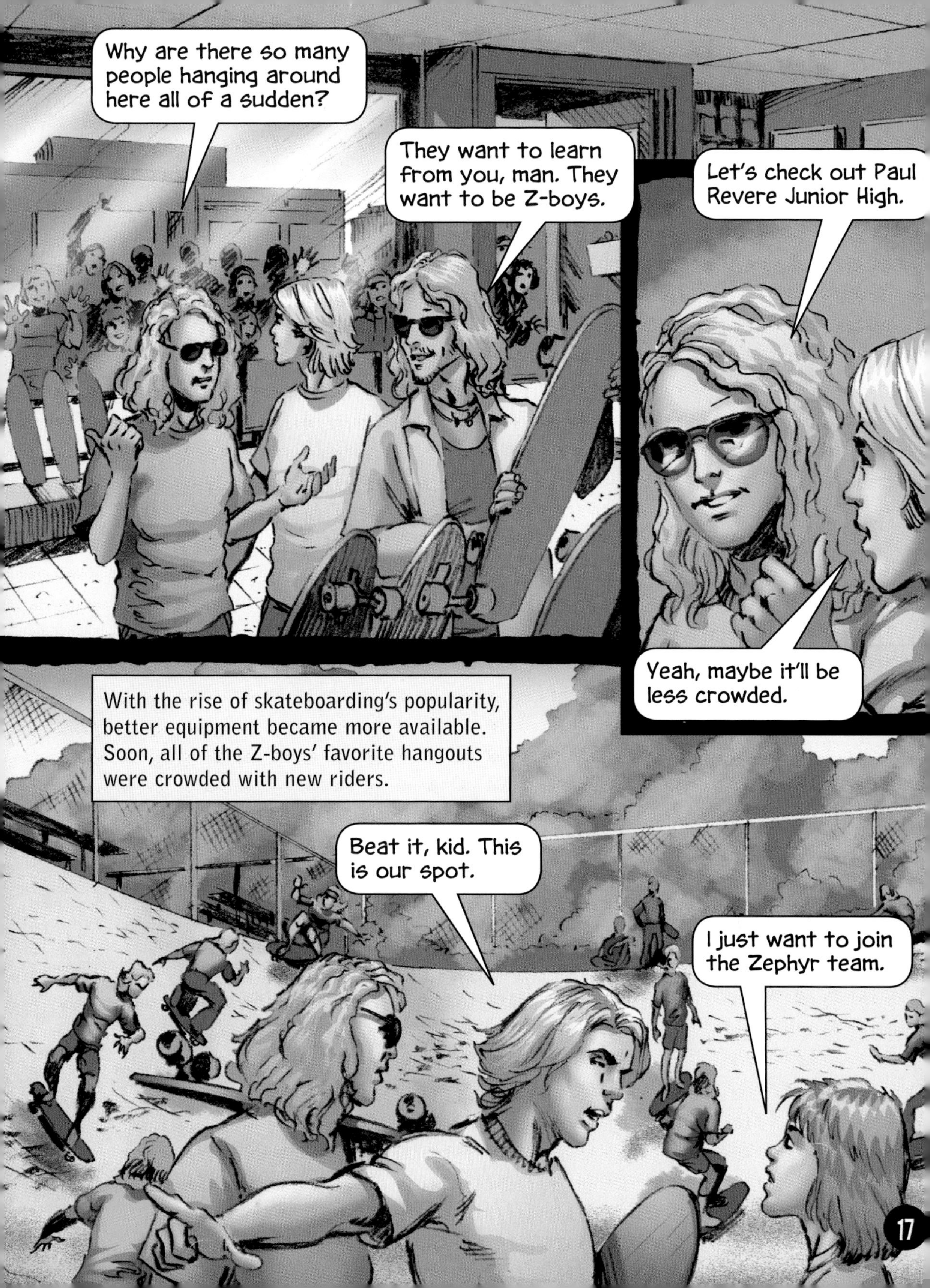
Why are there so many people hanging around here all of a sudden?
They want to learn from you, man. They want to be Z-boys.
Let's check out Paul Revere Junior High.
Yeah, maybe it'll be less crowded.
With the rise of skateboarding's popularity, better equipment became more available. Soon, all of the Z-boys' favorite hangouts were crowded with new riders.
Beat it, kid. This is our spot.
I just want to join the Zephyr team.

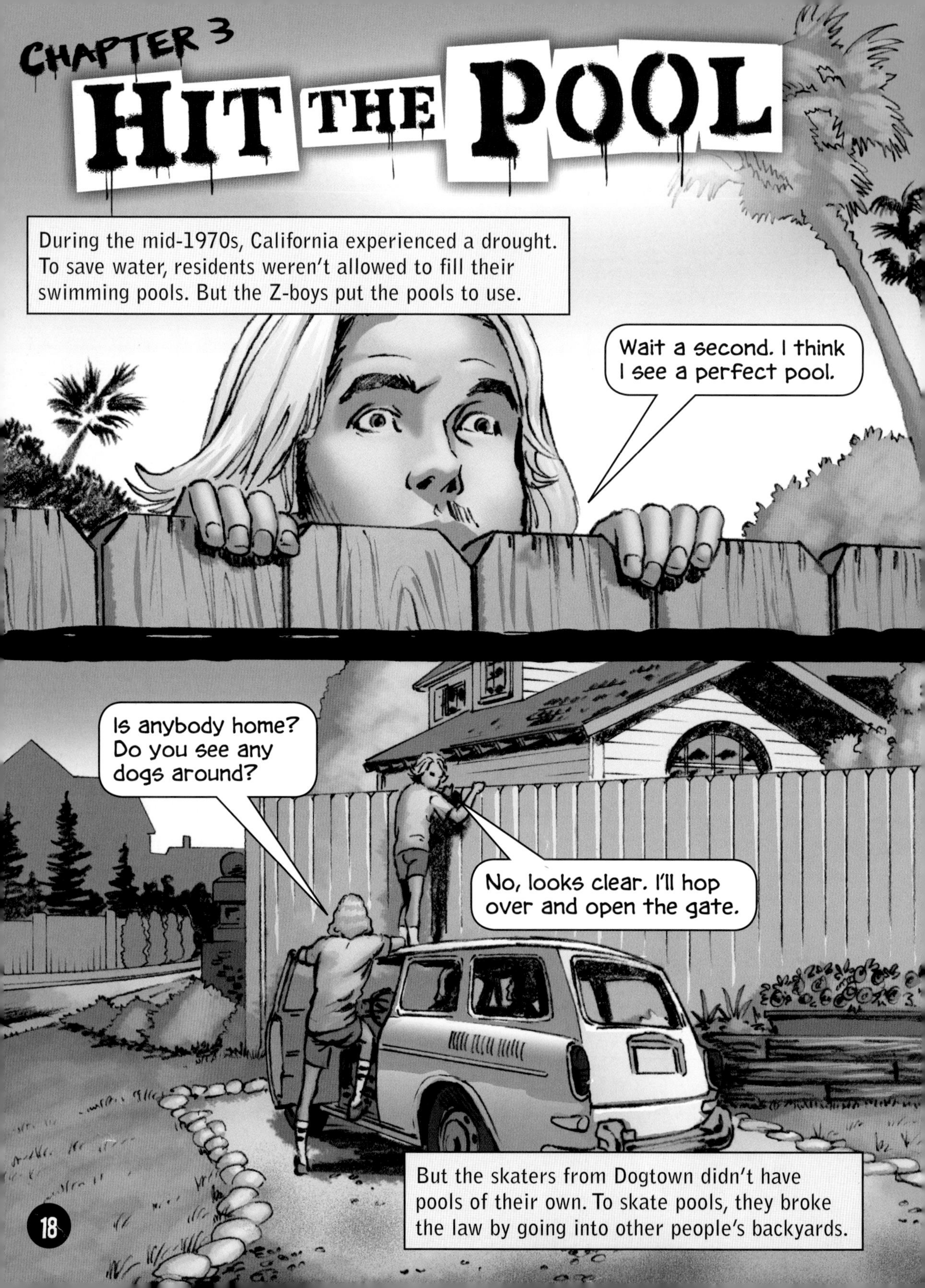
CHAPTER 3
HIT THE POOL
During the mid-1970s, California experienced a drought. To save water, residents weren't allowed to fill their swimming pools. But the Z-boys put the pools to use.
Wait a second. I think I see a perfect pool.
Is anybody home? Do you see any dogs around?
No, looks clear. I'll hop over and open the gate.
But the skaters from Dogtown didn't have pools of their own. To skate pools, they broke the law by going into other people's backyards.

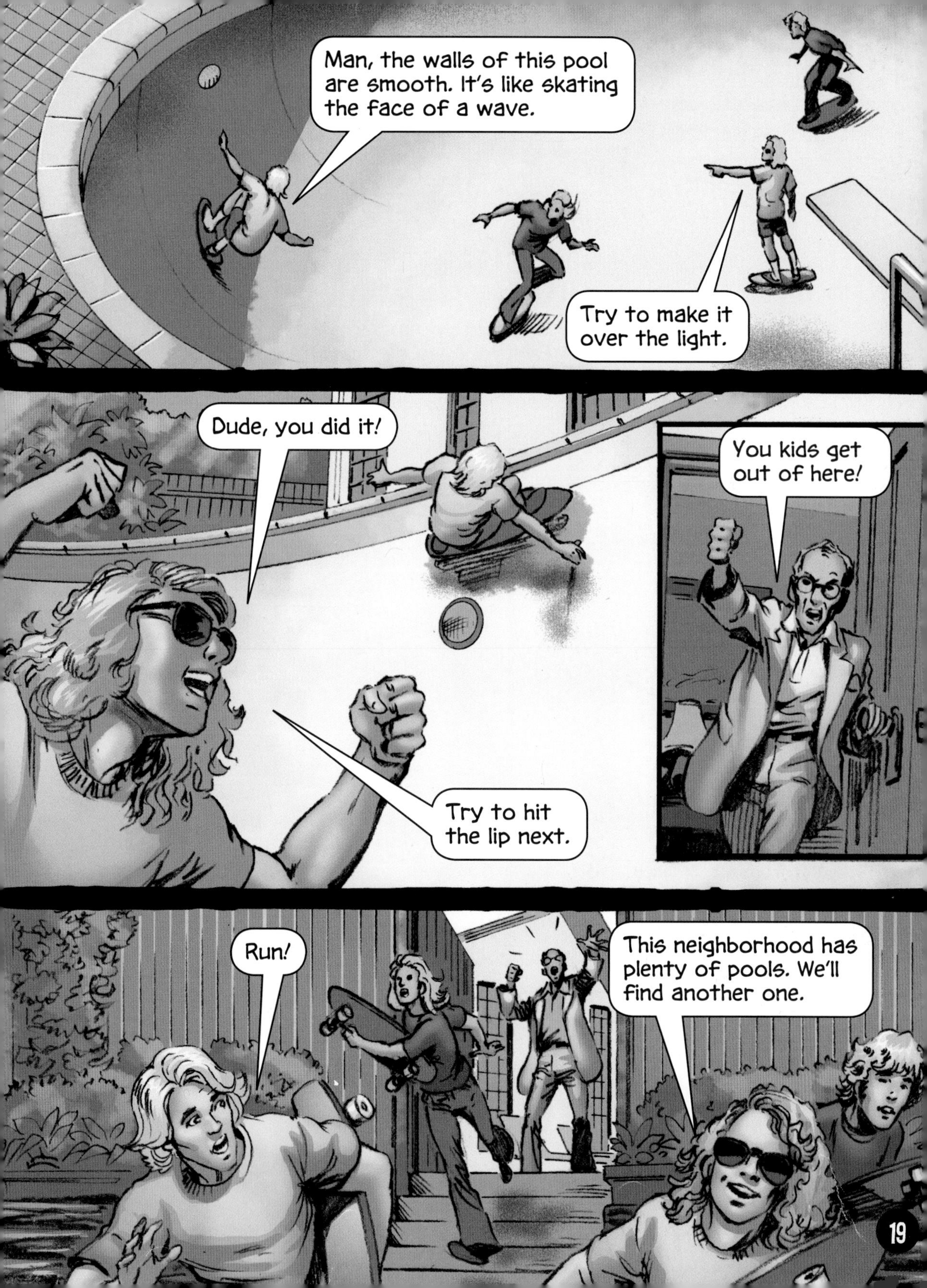
Man, the walls of this pool are smooth. It's like skating the face of a wave.
Try to make it over the light.
Dude, you did it!
Try to hit the lip next.
You kids get out of here!
Run!
This neighborhood has plenty of pools. We'll find another one.

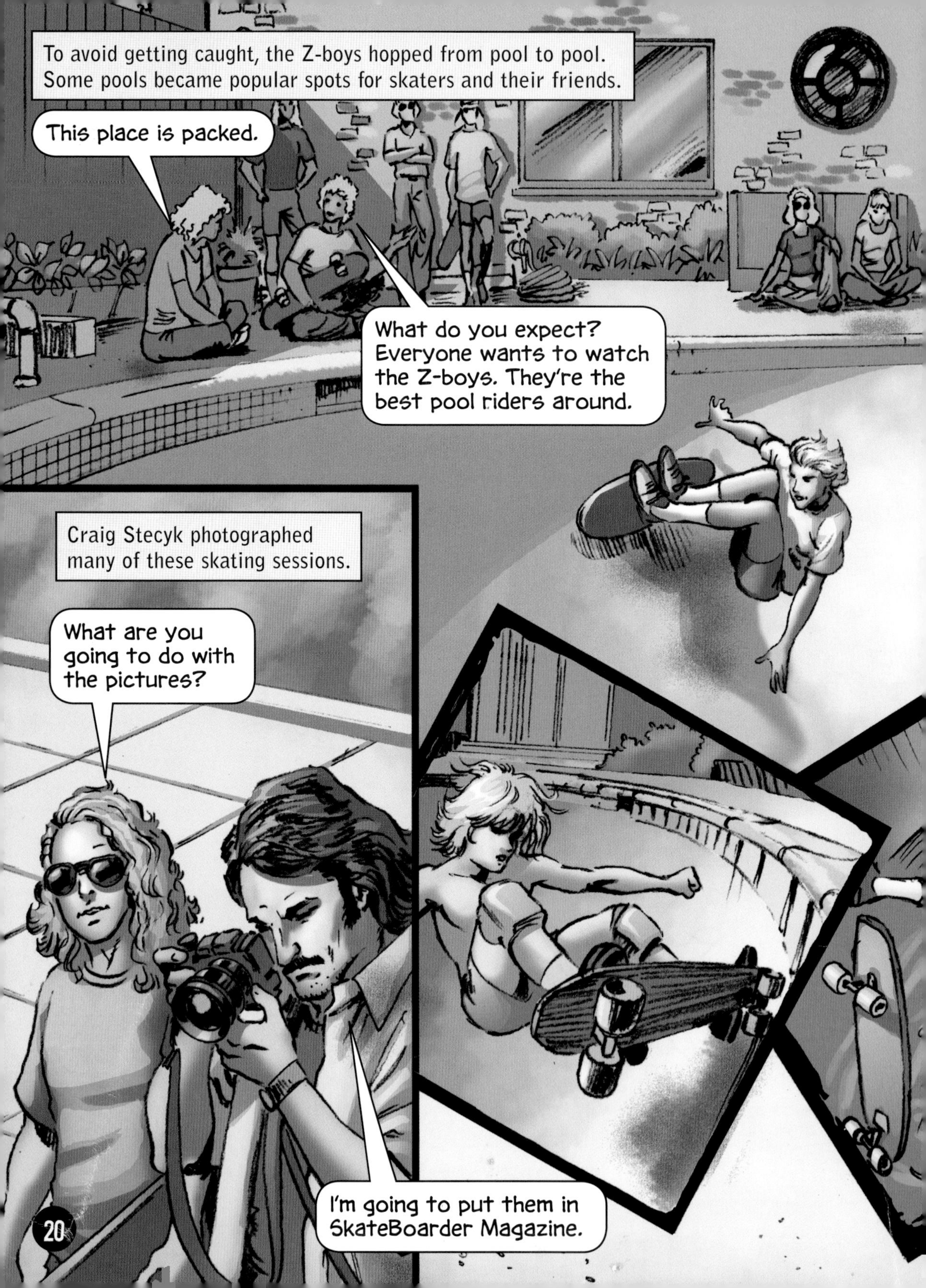
To avoid getting caught, the Z-boys hopped from pool to pool. Some pools became popular spots for skaters and their friends.
This place is packed.
What do you expect? Everyone wants to watch the Z-boys. They're the best pool riders around.
Craig Stecyk photographed many of these skating sessions.
What are you going to do with the pictures?
I'm going to put them in SkateBoarder Magazine.

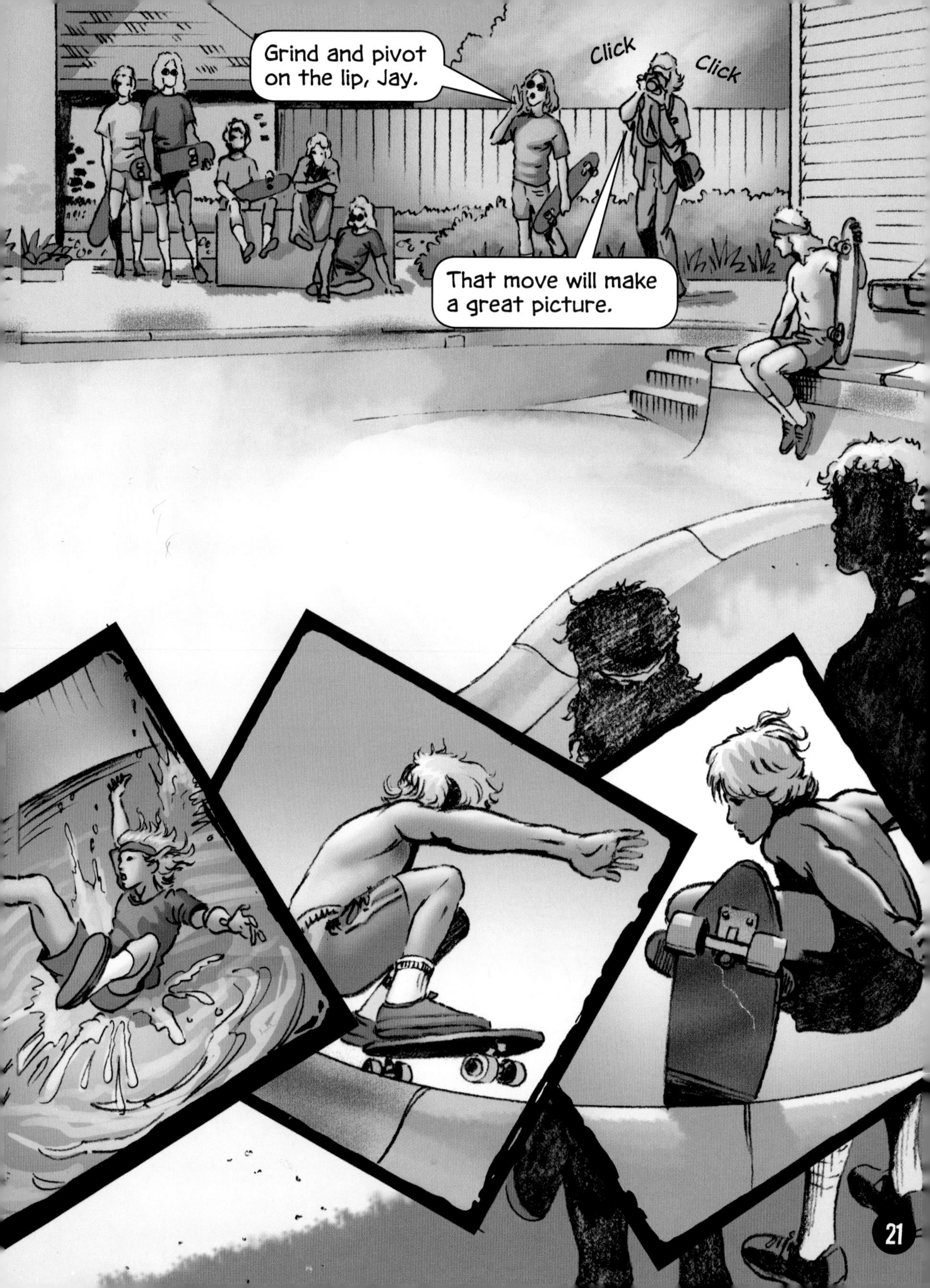

Grind and pivot on the lip, Jay.
Click
Click
That move will make a great picture.

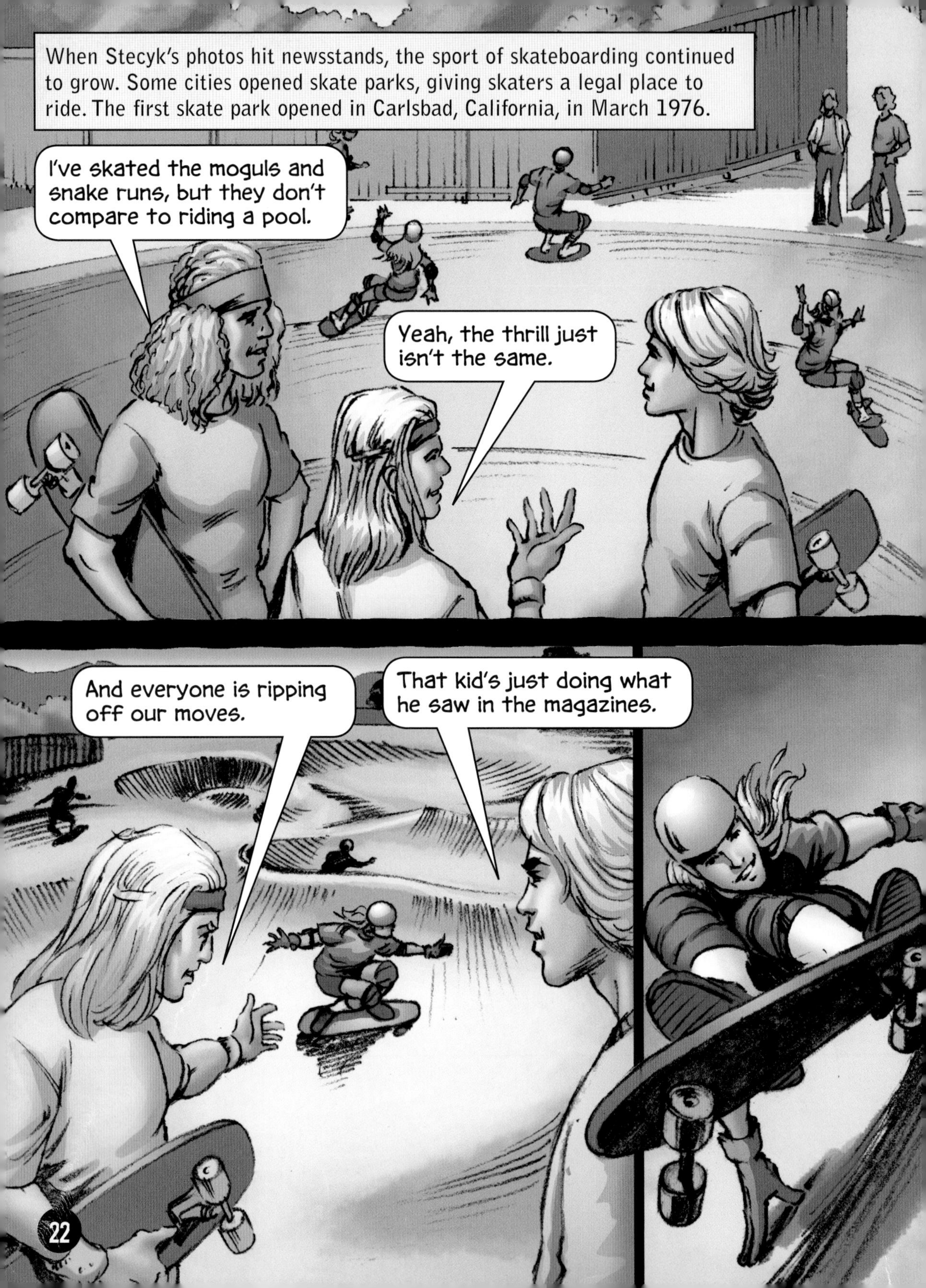
When Stecyk's photos hit newsstands, the sport of skateboarding continued to grow. Some cities opened skate parks, giving skaters a legal place to ride. The first skate park opened in Carlsbad, California, in March 1976.
I've skated the moguls and snake runs, but they don't compare to riding a pool.
Yeah, the thrill just isn't the same.
And everyone is ripping off our moves.
That kid's just doing what he saw in the magazines.

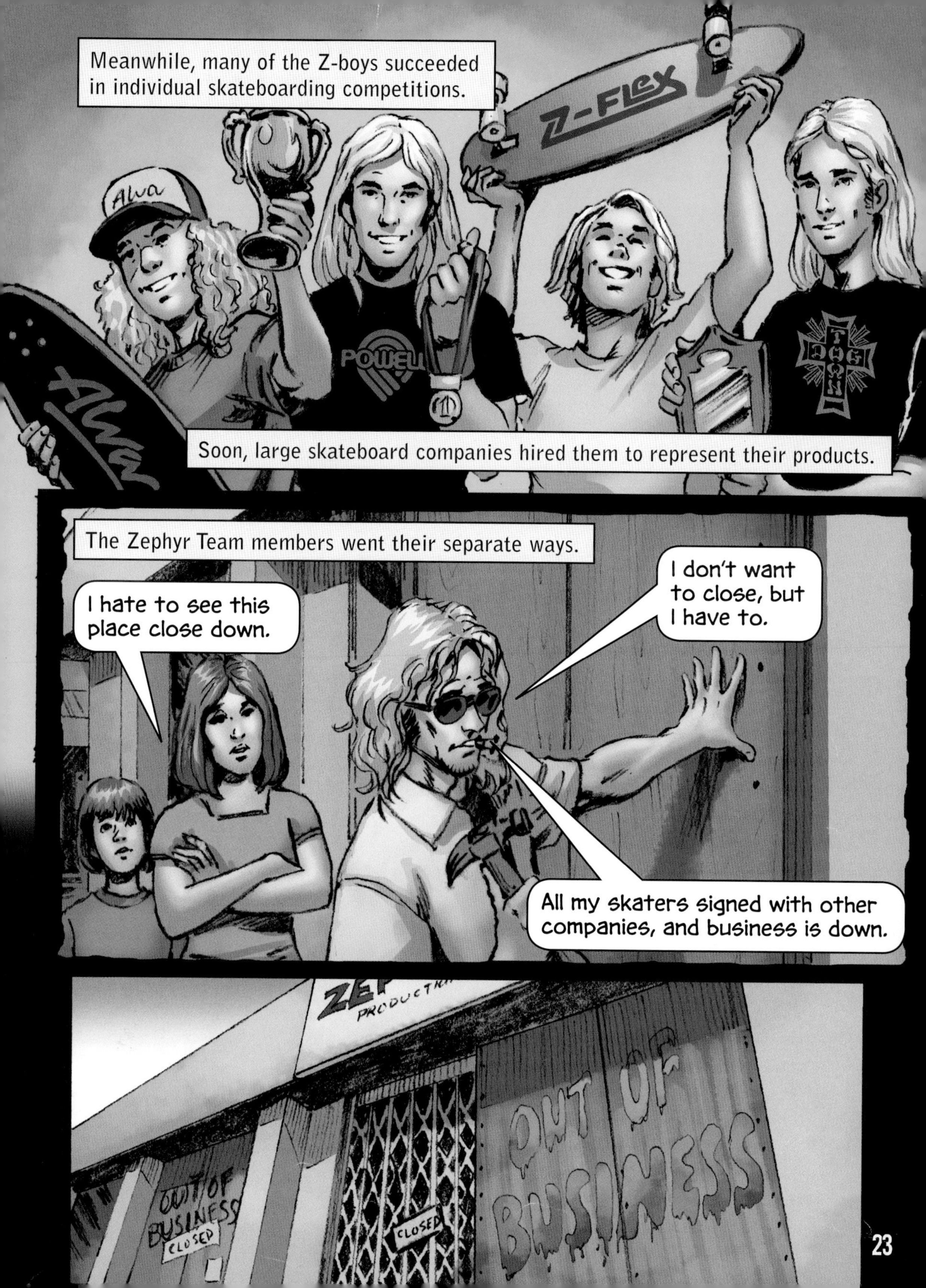
Meanwhile, many of the Z-boys succeeded in individual skateboarding competitions.
Alva
Z-FLEX
POWELL
Alva
Soon, large skateboard companies hired them to represent their products.
The Zephyr Team members went their separate ways.
I hate to see this place close down.
I don't want to close, but I have to.
All my skaters signed with other companies, and business is down.
OUT OF BUSINESS
CLOSED
CLOSED
OUT OF BUSINESS

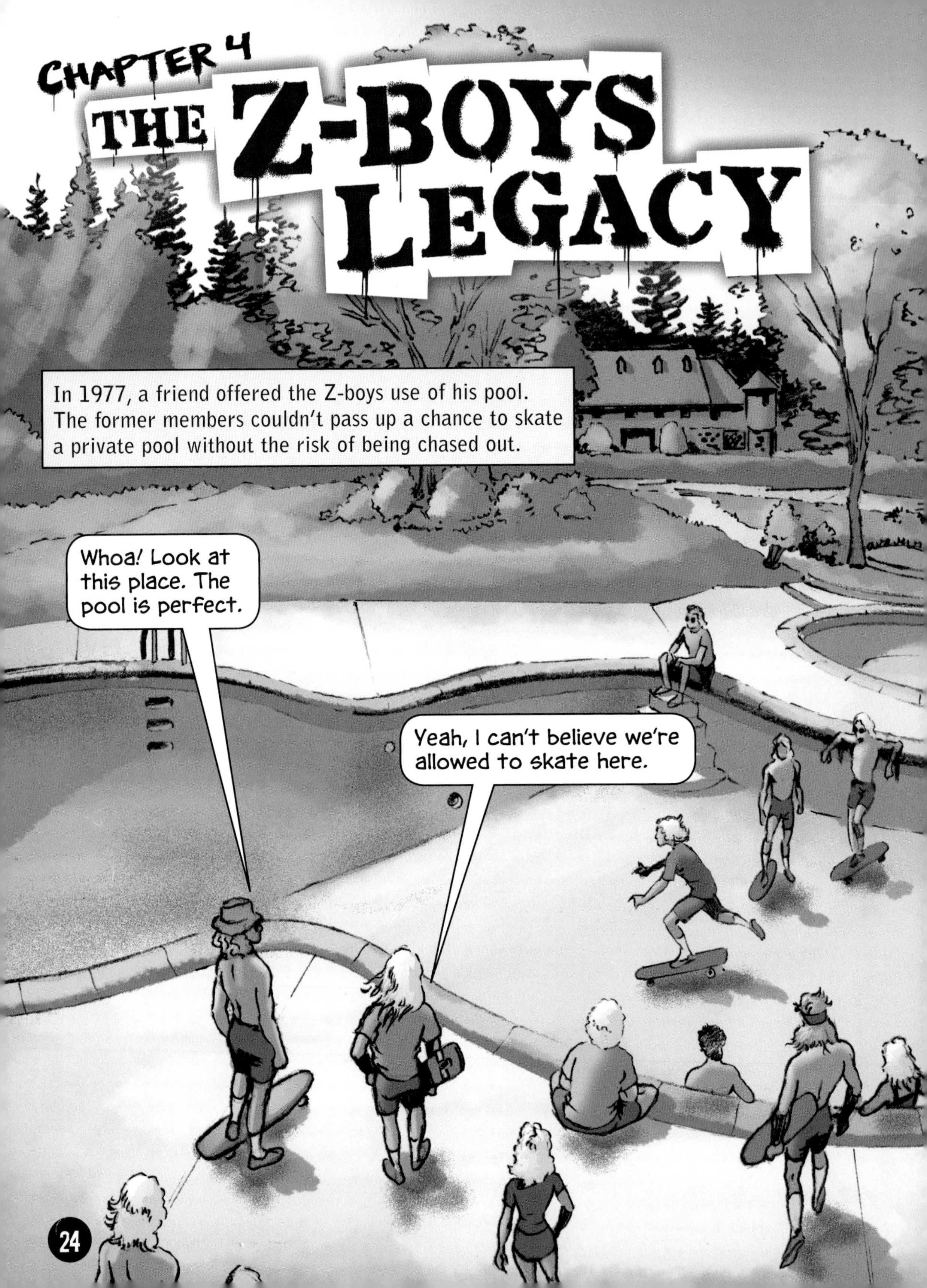
CHAPTER 4
THE Z-BOYS LEGACY
In 1977, a friend offered the Z-boys use of his pool. The former members couldn't pass up a chance to skate a private pool without the risk of being chased out.
Whoa! Look at this place. The pool is perfect.
Yeah, I can't believe we're allowed to skate here.

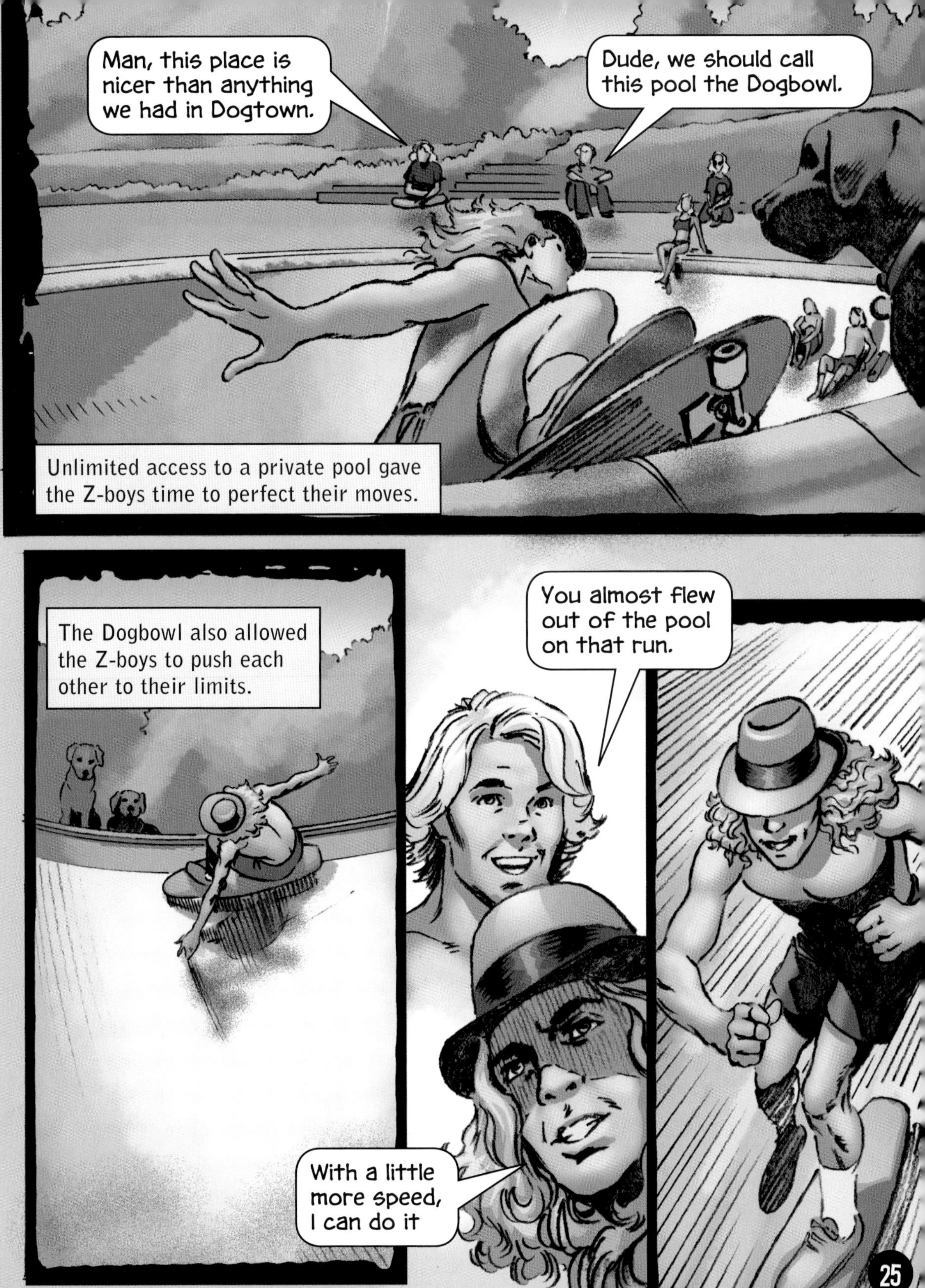
Man, this place is nicer than anything we had in Dogtown.
Dude, we should call this pool the Dogbowl.
Unlimited access to a private pool gave the Z-boys time to perfect their moves.
The Dogbowl also allowed the Z-boys to push each other to their limits.
You almost flew out of the pool on that run.
With a little more speed, I can do it

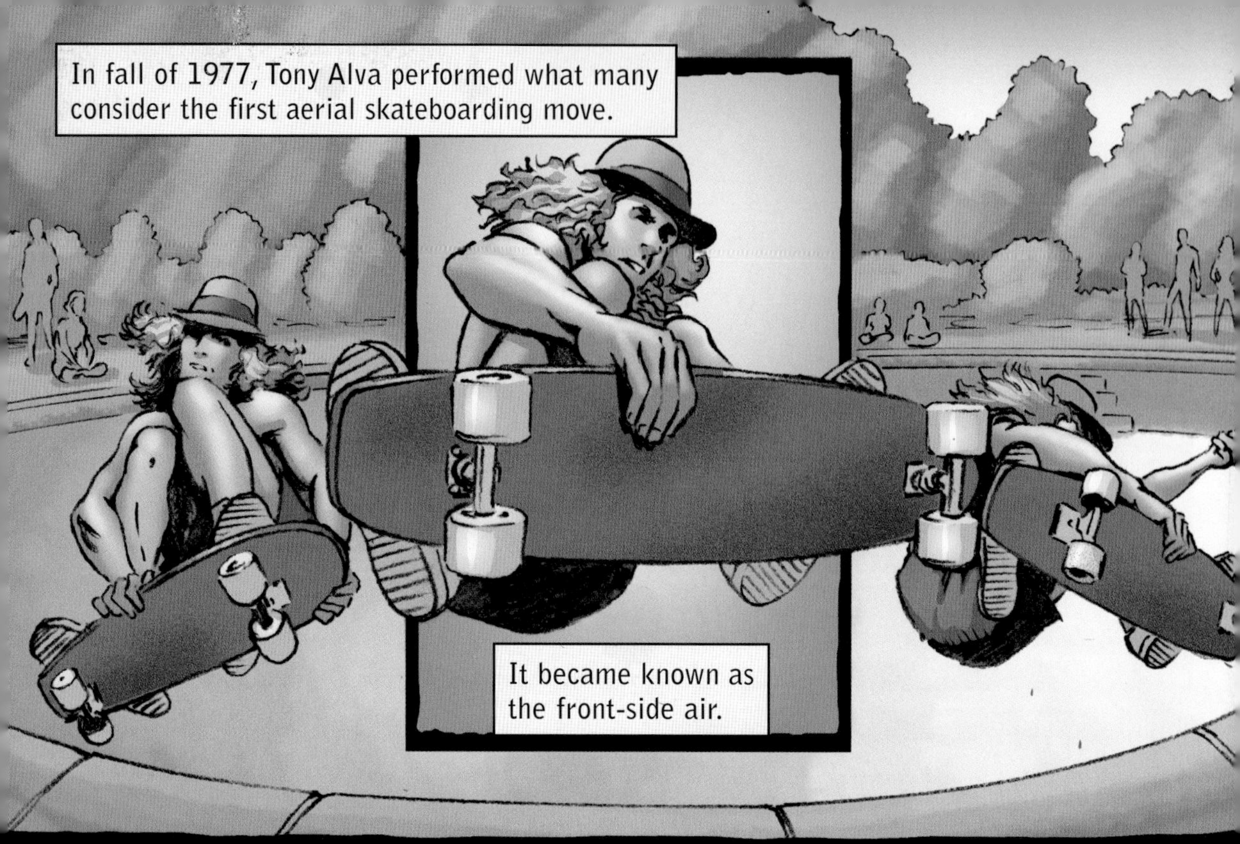
In fall of 1977, Tony Alva performed what many consider the first aerial skateboarding move.
It became known as the front-side air.

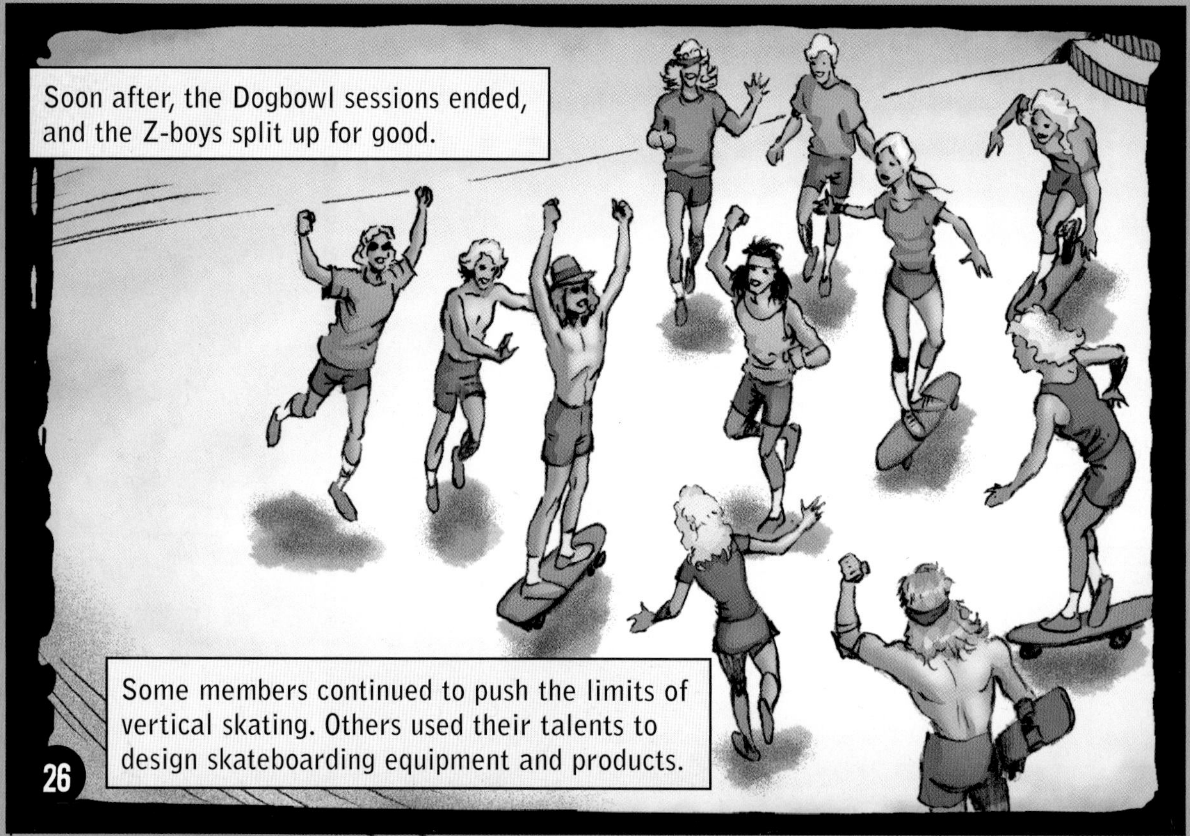
Soon after, the Dogbowl sessions ended, and the Z-boys split up for good.
Some members continued to push the limits of vertical skating. Others used their talents to design skateboarding equipment and products.

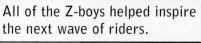

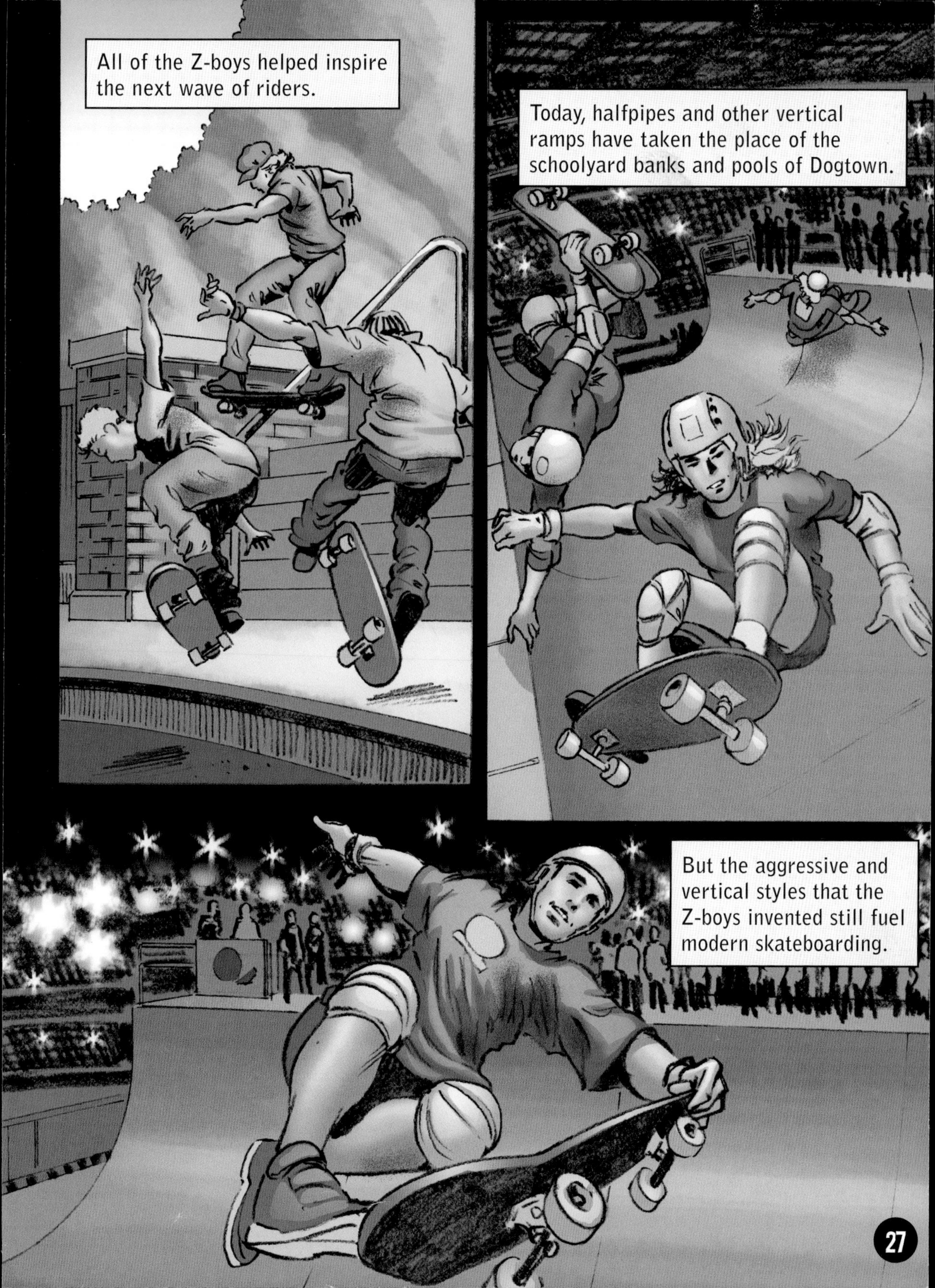

All of the Z-boys helped inspire the next wave of riders.

Today, halfpipes and other vertical ramps have taken the place of the schoolyard banks and pools of Dogtown.

But the aggressive and vertical styles that the Z-boys invented still fuel modern skateboarding.

# MORE ABOUT THE Z-BOYS AND SKATEBOARDING

- Former Z-boy Stacy Peralta went on to be a founding member of Powell Peralta skateboards. He learned skills as a filmmaker directing skateboarding videos. He later made a documentary about the Z-boys. Stacy Peralta's first signature skateboard sold 500 units per month.

- Tony Alva began his own company, selling Alva skateboards and clothing.

- Jay Adams continued to skate, but he also got in trouble with the law. He even spent time in jail. From jail, he wrote letters to skateboarding magazines encouraging kids to stay away from drugs.

- Through Stacy Peralta's *Bones Brigade* videos for Powell Peralta, a young skater named Tony Hawk became popular. Today, he credits Peralta for helping him become a famous skater.

- Peggy Oki went to college to study biology. She is an artist and an environmentalist.

- By 1976, the Z-boys had helped turn skateboarding into a $400 million industry.

- For the past 30 years, Tony Alva has never gone more than a few days without riding a skateboard.

- Vertical skating has been a official X Games competition since the first X Games were held in 1995.

- The 2005 movie, *Lords of Dogtown* was based on the lives of the Z-Boys. Stacy Peralta wrote the screenplay.

# GLOSSARY

**aerial** (AIR-ee-uhl)—a trick that is performed in the air

**asphalt** (ASS-fawlt)—a black tar that is mixed with sand and gravel to make paved roads

**carve** (KARV)—to make sharp turns on a surfboard or skateboard without skidding

**drought** (DROUT)—a long period with little or no rainfall

**freestyle** (FREE-stile)—a skateboarding style that includes many gymnastics moves

**urethane** (YUR-uh-thayn)—a hard plastic used to make skateboard wheels

# INTERNET SITES

FactHound offers a safe, fun way to find Internet sites related to this book. All of the sites on FactHound have been researched by our staff.

Here's how:
1. Visit *www.facthound.com*
2. Choose your grade level.
3. Type in this book ID **1429601507** for age-appropriate sites. You may also browse subjects by clicking on letters, or by clicking on pictures and words.
4. Click on the **Fetch It** button.

**FactHound will fetch the best sites for you!**

# READ MORE

Crossingham, John, and Bobbie Kalman. *Extreme Skateboarding.* Extreme Sports No Limits. New York: Crabtree, 2004.

Doeden, Matt. *Skateboarding.* To the Extreme. Mankato, Minn.: Capstone Press, 2005.

Noll, Rhyn. *Skateboarding: Past-Present-Future.* Atglen, Penn.: Schiffer, 2003.

Preszler, Eric. *Skateboarding.* X-Sports. Mankato, Minn.: Capstone Press, 2005.

# BIBLIOGRAPHY

Brown, Emerson. "Stacy Peralta on Dogtown and Z-Boys." http://www.switchmagazine.com/skateboard_storys/dogtown_zboys.html.

*Dogtown and Z-Boys: The Birth of Extreme.* DVD, directed by Stacy Peralta. (2001; Culver City, CA: Columbia TriStar, 2005.)

The First Z-boys Presence on the Internet. http://www.angelfire.com/ca2/dtown/.

Ruibal, Sal. "Cutting Edge Sports Trace Roots Back to 1970s." http://www.usatoday.com/sports/other/2002-04-17-cover-extreme.htm.

Stecyk, Craig. *Dogtown: The Legend of the Z-Boys.* New York: Burning Flags Press, 2000.

# INDEX